Specter Grimoire: A Guide to Spells, Witchcraft and Tarot

Jessica Specter

Lavender Moon Media, LLC.

Also by Jessica Specter

Specter Thriller Collection (a Lavender Moon Media, LLC.

Production)

All About Bears (a Bear Grounds Coffee Co. Production)

ISBN: 979-8-3303-0866-8

To Cerberus, my fawn doberman.

Table of Contents

Specter Grimoire: A Guide to Spells, Witchcraft and Tarot

Author's Note

I am happy you found this piece of literature to aid you in your spiritual journey. Whether you are a beginner or seasoned, this will serve as an almanac of guidance to reflect on when conducting your own personally crafted spells and practice.

I am creating this for you, as I wish I had reliable guidance like this when I started out. Much of the books I saw over-the-counter seemed over the top and "salesy." That's not to say that they *wouldn't* have worked because I didn't try them - but I did not trust them. To each their own.

Everything I know has been garnered from my 10 years (and counting if you're reading this) of personal experience. My biggest affinity has always been tarot, as some of you may know, considering my original decks. However, you will find a multitude of useful information that I too use and flip through when needed. Happy spell casting!

A General Grimoire

Oh boy, where to start… You can start with your own deck of tarot cards. It can really be that simple. Try not to overcomplicate things, is my word of advice to you. For the newbies: The advice and information provided will be the foundation and building blocks for everything going forward on your journey. Good luck!

Colors

This is a huge underlying component of witchcraft that you will find seeping its way into practically everything. Much of what we use for spells, what you see in tarot cards and more can be interpreted or chosen simply via color.

Pink: Love, compassion, emotional healing, affection, nurturing and romance. Gentleness, kindness and unconditional love.

Green: Growth, renewal, harmony, balance, prosperity, healing, nature and fertility. Abundance in all forms such as financial wealth and emotional well-being.

Blue: Serenity, peace, tranquility, communication, truth, wisdom and spiritual connection. Calmness, clarity of thought and depth.

Yellow: Happiness, optimism, intellect, creativity, clarity and joy. Agility, communication and enhancing logical thinking.

Black: Mystery, the unknown, protection, absorption and repelling of negative energy and transformation. It can also symbolize the hidden or subconscious aspects of the self.

White: Purity, innocence, spirituality, truth, peace and illumination. Higher realms, divine presence and clarity.

Purple: Spirituality, intuition, psychic abilities, wisdom, royalty, magic and transformation. Connection with higher realms and spiritual fulfillment.

Red: Passion, energy, vitality, courage, love and action. Life force, survival instincts and physicality.

Orange: Creativity, enthusiasm, vitality, success, attraction and energy. Warmth, positivity and zest for life.

Gold: Wealth, prosperity, abundance, success, achievement and illumination. Protection and spiritual enlightenment.

Silver: Intuition, introspection, insight, reflection, lunar energy and feminine energy. Psychic abilities and mystical aspects.

Brown: Grounding, stability, reliability, strength, security and earth connection. Practicality, material matters and physical comfort.

Crystals

Crystals can and are used for a variety of purposes depending on their attributes. They can assist with healing, meditation, energy clearing, protection, manifestation, chakra balancing, divination and chakra balancing. Here are some common stones and their purposes:

Clear Quartz: A versatile stone used to amplify energy and intentions. It can also be used for clarity, purification, enhancing spiritual awareness and connecting with higher realms.

Rose Quartz: Used for love, compassion and emotional healing. It can attract love, promote self-love, foster forgiveness and harmony in relationships.

Citrine: Abundance, prosperity and success. It can manifest wealth, promote positivity, enhance creativity and self-confidence.

Jade: Purity and serenity. Promotes peace, wisdom and healing.

Black Tourmaline: Repels negative energies. Can be used for grounding, purification and creating security.

Tiger's Eye: Protective against psychic attacks and negative energies. Promotes courage, strength and confidence.

Lapis Lazuli: For wisdom, truth and spiritual awareness. It stimulates intellect, enhances intuition and aids in the spiritual journey.

Selenite: Cleanses and purifies. Brings mental peace and clarity. Used for meditation, spiritual growth and connecting with higher realms/beings.

Aventurine: Luck, prosperity and opportunity. Manifests abundance, enhances creativity and promotes balance/optimism.

Obsidian: Absorbs negative energies and shields against psychic attacks. Promotes grounding, self-reflection and releasing emotional blockages.

Labradorite: Enhances intuition, psychic abilities and spiritual awakening. It protects the aura, strengthens faith in oneself and aids in spiritual transformation.

Opal: Inspiration, enhances creativity and imagination.

Ruby: Vitality, passion and life force. Enhances energy, courage and motivation. Prosperity, success and abundance in ventures.

Diamond: Clarity, purity and high vibration. Cosmic consciousness, strength, invincibility and fearlessness.

Emerald: Heart-centric, promoting love, compassion and harmony. Enhances loyalty, unity and friendship.

Amethyst: Enhances psychic abilities, spiritual wisdom/growth and connecting with higher consciousness.

Other Materials

Pearl: Tapping into inner wisdom and nurturing love. Enhances integrity, brings about truth and inhibits immodest behavior.

Blood: Life, vitality, binding, offerings, activating agent for spells/tools/talismans.

Bone: Strength, structure, durability, divination uses, protection and offerings/ritual tools.

Feather: Spiritual communication, air element, protection, warding and offerings. Different feathers have different uses/meanings.

How to Cleanse, Charge and Empower Crystals

A simple way to cleanse a crystal is by running water over it. Make sure your crystal can be immersed in water before doing so. If it is a more fragile stone, consider smoking it with incense or sound (bells, singing bowls, snapping your fingers, etc.).

To charge your crystals, you can set them outside during the night of a full Moon. To charge them with earth energy, you can place them in plants within your yard/house.

To set your intention, choose a stone that correlates with your manifestation desire. Calm your mind and hold it between your closed hands. Imagine the stone's energy flowing up through your body during deep-breathing exercises. You may also speak your intentions to it. Visualize your manifestation occurring. You may keep your crystal with you or place it in a safe spot.

Plants

Plants are commonly used in witchcraft and spells. This pertains to green magic, but it is not exclusive. Here are the fundamental ones for your baseline of knowledge:

Lavender: Calming, relaxation and purification. Spells for peace and healing.

Rosemary: Protection, purification and memory enhancement. Used for clarity and mental focus.

Sage: Cleansing and purification. Burned to clear negative energies (similar to incense).

Mugwort: Divination and prophetic dreams. Used in spells and rituals for psychic abilities/astral projection.

Thyme: Courage, strength and healing. Used for courage and energy.

Chamomile: Calming. Used for sleep, meditation and relaxation.

Cinnamon: Prosperity, success and protection. Used in spells for wealth and enhancing personal power.

Patchouli: Attracts love, wealth and grounding energy. Used for prosperity and romance.

Yarrow: Protection and divination. Used to enhance psychic abilities and for love spells.

Mistletoe: Fertility, protection and healing. Used for love and protection.

Bay Leaf: Protection, manifesting and purification.

Proven Science on Plants:

Plants affect humans psychologically and physiologically. Their simple presence aids us physically by…

- Decreasing the level of cortisol (stress hormone) in your body, decreasing stress and anxiety.

- Improve air quality by absorbing and filtering toxins.

- Reduces pain and aids wounds in healing quicker.

- Increasing the number of white blood cells (your warrior blood cells that fight off viruses/heal you/etc).

Plants aid us psychologically and socially by…

- Reducing aggression, increasing social cohesion, improved mood and wellbeing.

- Increased job satisfaction.

- Increased socialization.

- Eliciting feelings of empowerment

Other benefits found are sound absorption (by the Ficus plant), improved focus and increased humidity (the Spider Plant specifically). The Peace Lily plant is also known to filter the air of formaldehyde, benzene and carbon monoxide (Niazi, P., Alimyar, O., Azizi, A., Monib, A. W., & Ozturk, H.).

Plants can sense the world around them. How, you ask? Venus fly trap. There was also a study conducted by WSU in which they found plants can sense varying pressure when touched (Howell, A. H., Völkner, C., McGreevy, P.).

Candles

Candles are used during rituals and spells to aid in the manifestation of one's desire. I view candles similarly as I do crystals - I do not think they make the entirety of the spell, but they aid in it. It's like adding an extra "oomf".

Candles come in different colors and you use different ones for your goal/s. Refer back to our "Colors" section to guide you on your selection. If you plan to practice magic for a long time I suggest you just buy them in all the colors.

Some practitioners recommend burning the candles down completely. If you choose to go this route, use the stick ones or use birthday candles, as they are small. However, I extinguished the candles after the completion of my rituals and found they still worked. If you are re-using a candle, cleanse it first. It is your preference. In some cases, such as binding spells with two candle sticks signifying two people, I do recommend that you burn them completely.

Scents

You may use scents in your spells to enhance your results or use them as offerings. I like to use essential oils as well. Besides a few that can be found underneath the 'Plants' section, take a look at some more scents and their uses:

Sandalwood: Calmness, peace and relaxation. Used for love, healing, purification and sleep spells.

Rose: Love, beauty and attraction. Used for love, harmony, emotional healing and self-love spells.

Frankincense: Spiritual awareness, purification and meditation. Used for protection and spirituality.

Patchouli: Grounding and stabilizing. Used for prosperity, fertility and attracting abundance.

Cedarwood: Strength, courage and purification. Used for protection, grounding and prosperity.

Peppermint: Mental clarity and purification. Used for healing, psychic awareness and purification.

Myrrh: Spirituality, meditation and healing. Used for protection and purification.

Ylang Ylang: Relaxation, sensuality and attraction. Used for love, peace and harmony.

Tools for Divination

Within this section you will be introduced to various tools and methods of divination. It includes but is not limited to the styles mentioned. There should be more than enough variation here to find the perfect one for your practice.

Pendulum

A mathematically even object suspended by a chain, wire, etc. This divination tool can be used for "yes or no" questions. You may also utilize a paper/mat with different answers underneath it for the pendulum to sway toward.

You use a pendulum by first focusing your energy and clearing your mind. Then, suspend the pendulum in the air, in the center of either question. Or, you can say that one direction is for "yes" and the opposite is for "no". Then, without forcing it to move in a particular direction and holding it steady, allow it to reveal the answer to you.

Ouija Boards

You have to know this one! I stay away from this personally. My first time trying it was with a friend during a beach staycation in Florida.

We had created our own Ouija board out of paper and used a penny as the centerpiece. Very bootleg but keep in mind we were around 13 years old and didn't have money for Ouija boards, nor would our parents probably buy us one.

It worked, to say the least. At first I thought my friend was moving it on purpose just to make it "seem real". Then I decided to do it on my own to see if it would move. I watched and waited for it to move for about twenty seconds and was starting to tell my friend how it was fake before it began to *pull itself* across the paper, I could *feel the pulling*, and I freaked out.

So yes it works, no I have not tried it again since. However if you want to do it here are some dos and don'ts:

Do:

1. Only take your hands off of the centerpiece once you reach "Goodbye".

2. Stay calm and be in a calm environment that won't be disturbed.

3. Protect yourself before and after.

4. State your intention to only speak with positive entities/whichever entities you would wish to speak to.

5. Have a plan of questions to ask.

6. Approach the session openly but cautiously.

7. Preferably utilize an Ouija board in a group setting.

Don't:

1. Show disrespect toward entities.

2. Lift your hands off of the centerpiece.

3. Force movement.

4. Ask provocative questions.

5. Use in negative places.

6. Share personal information.

Entities to be Wary of:

I literally feel a chill going down my spine. I don't even want to write the name. As I am coming again to write it I feel that same chill so I am not saying it. Please do your research and look up various bad entities and their names that can pop up before you use one so you are prepared.

Negative entities and demons are able to communicate with you through this. You are opening a door quite literally, which is why it's important to always go to "Goodbye" when you're finished.

Be careful if an entity keeps switching up their answers. For instance, if you ask, "How old are you?" and they say 12, and then later 9, end the session. These entities can try to play tricks on you or pretend to be good.

Runes

Originating from Norse religion. These different symbols represent various meanings, and for some, deities.

The History of Runes

I just learned this due to the research I'm doing. I previously thought runes were only used by Norse people and Vikings. Disclaimer: I'm partially Scandinavian. Well, it turns out I am even more heavily connected to this form of craft because it also includes people from England and Wales. It also includes Denmark, Germany and other parts of Germanic Europe.

The earliest inscriptions can be found in Germany, Scandinavia and Denmark. The oldest inscription was found on a medallion in Denmark. Runes are a part of the Elder Futhark alphabet.

Did you know there's more than one style of runic alphabet? Elder Futhark (24 characters, starting from 1 to

250 A.D. to 800 A.D.) is the oldest. There is also Anglo-Saxon Futhorc (400 to 1100 A.D., between 26 and 33 letters) and Younger Futhark (800 to 1100 A.D., 16 characters). I will be discussing Elder Futhark

Personal experience insertion

I created the logo for Specter, as you see on the cover of this book, around 2020. I wanted a logo that looked cool with some interesting line work. The goal was to create something unisex with a hint of "badass-ery". At that time I never used runes or looked into them.

I've honestly had a handful of people say it looks demonic, but at the same time they are super Christian people and they probably wouldn't be interested in tarot cards or things like this grimoire anyway, so, womp womp. This logo is for the people who get it. Also there are plenty of other brands that have horned animals that aren't viewed that way, but I digress. Ahem.

When I defined Specter's brand, I stated our core values to be originality, strength, perseverance, perception and quality. I also stated, "Specter encompasses the belief that art is not only a medium for creative expression, but also a powerful tool for challenging preconceived notions and exploring the complexities of life. Specializing in the artistic style of surrealism, which serves to encourage viewers to look beyond the surface, discover hidden truths and the beauty in the world around us.

The mission is to showcase the raw, unfiltered aspects of life through this unique style and to inspire others to embrace their own creativity and authenticity. I believe that nothing is as it seems. By embracing the paradoxes and contradictions of life we can discover a deeper understanding of ourselves and the world we inhabit. Join me on this journey of self-discovery and artistic exploration, where the blunt and beautiful are celebrated in equal measure."

It wouldn't be until later on in 2023 when I was finished working on my first two tarot decks that I would notice a correlation. I was doing personal research on runes. I already made some the year prior out of clay and paint, but I was doing a deep dive.

For some reason it didn't click until then. I noticed that Algiz looks a lot - wait - *exactly* like the line work in the Specter logo. I had to read more about this symbol. Sure enough, the Algiz rune encompassed the brand I was trying to embody. What are the odds?

Algiz

The fifteenth rune in Futhark (Germanic spelling used by Scandinavians and Anglo-Saxons). It symbolizes the worlds of life and death with the rainbow bridge.

Translation: Elk

Magical use: Defense against enemies and protection of you and those you love.

Meanings: Protection, defense, awakening, higher life, connection with the divine, strength, fortitude, instinct, communication and message. Other sources state "strength in the face of suffering - withstanding despite certain death" and banishment of opposing forces.

Interestingly enough, my Bachelor's degree is in Communication (No, Communication is not just a degree in talking). It was a coincidence that Algiz is within the Specter logo. It is a coincidence that is now embraced, accepted and embodied. You have to admit that it fits perfectly. I hope that all the products sold embossed with this logo provide the people who hold them with protection.

How to Use

There are a variety of ways to utilize runes in your divination and spiritual practice. I consider their uses similar to sigils in some ways, which we will touch on later.

For divination, you can ask a question and draw a rune, or spread, for the answer. You can carve, draw or inscribe runes with your desired effect on objects. Traditional methods of utilizing runes were to protect, do spell work, curse, predict the future, imbue objects or conjure.

You can use **bind runes**, which are a combination of two or more runes for an effect including each rune's meaning. **Radial bind runes** are commonly used in defense spells, protection spells and amulets.

Meanings in Numerical Order

1. Fehu

Meaning: Wealth/Cattle/Livestock

Deities: Freya, Freyr or Njord.

Upright: Wealth, abundance, success, reward or increase.

Reversed: Financial worries, bankruptcy, loss or fall from grace.

1. Uruz -

Meaning: Aurochs (wild ox)

Deities: Thor.

Upright: Survival, endurance, physical power, independence, life force.

Reversed: Weak willpower, lack of motivation and missed opportunities.

2. Thurisaz -

Meaning: Giants

Deities: Thor.

Upright: Strong, conflict, tool/weapon, defense, violence and protection.

Reversed: Irritation, hidden fears and internal struggles.

3. Ansuz -

Meaning: A God

Deities: Loki or Odin.

Upright: Communication, order, inspiration, breath and blessing.

Reversed: Miscommunication, imbalance and insincerity.

4. Raidho -

Meaning: Ride

Upright: Travel, spiritual path or progress.

Reversed: Panic, bad intuition or procrastination.

5. Kennaz -

Meaning: Torch

Deities: Freya.

Upright: Knowledge, controlled fire, hearth and experience.

Reversed: Ignorance, delays and failures.

6. Gebo -

Meaning: Gift

Deities: Freya or Odin.

Upright: Gifts, sacred union, generosity, innate talent, relationships or reciprocity.

Reversed: N/A

7. Wunjo -

Meaning: Joy

Deities: Odin or Freya.

Upright: Hope, friendship, family, harmony, hope or pleasure.

Reversed: Misfortune, disappointment or hard times.

8. Hagalaz -

Meaning: Hail

Deities: Balder.

Upright: Transformation, freedom, awakening, catastrophe, surrender, opportunity, crisis and radical change.

Reversed: N/A

9. Nauthiz -

Meaning: Need

Upright: Endurance, necessity, restraint, urgency and life lessons.

Reversed: N/A

10. Isa -

Meaning: Ice

Deities: Freya.

Upright: Stasis, stillness, introspection, blocks or self control.

Reversed: N/A

11. Jera -

Meaning: Year

Deities: Freyr or Freya.

Upright: Harvest, orbits, time, patience, prosperity and growth.

Reversed: N/A

12. Eihwaz -

Meaning: Yew tree

Deities: Odin.

Upright: Endings, death, timeless, immortality, guardian and initiation.

Reversed: N/A

13. Perthro -

Meaning: Lot Cup/Dice Cup

Upright: Luck, fate, play, games, divination, secrets and mysteries.

Reversed: Caution, instability, misfortune and dishonesty.

14. Algiz -

Meaning: Elk

Upright: Protection, higher self, divinity, spiritual connection, success, luck and life force.

Reversed: N/A

15. Sowilo -

Meaning: Sun

Deities: Balder or Thor.

Upright: Victory, guidance, security, wholeness, power and self-confidence.

Reversed: N/A

16. Tiwaz -

Meaning: Star

Deities: Thor.

Upright: Bravery, justice, sacrifice, laws, principles, war and honor.

Reversed: Giving up too soon.

17. Berkana -

Meaning: Birch

Deities: Hel or Frigg.

Upright: Rebirth, sanctuary, healing, safety and creation.

Reversed: Sterility, stagnation and lack of ideas.

18. Ehwaz -

Meaning: Horse

Deities: Freyr or Freya.

Upright: Travel, teamwork, love, animals and partnership.

Reversed: Lack of trust and conflicts.

19. Mannaz -

Meaning: Mankind

Deities: Odin.

Upright: Mind, learning, intelligence and humanity.

Reversed: Close-minded and isolated.

20. Laguz -

Meaning: Lake

Deities: Balder or Njord.

Upright: Collective memory, psychic powers, dreams, unity and imagination.

Reversed: Lack of imagination, self-doubt or procrastination.

21. Inguz -

Meaning: Seed

Deities: Ing or Freyr.

Upright: Creation, genesis, fertility, energy, children and love.

Reversed: N/A

22. Othala -

Meaning: Homeland

Deities: Odin or Thor.

Upright: Home, ancestors, family, legacy, inheritance or

heaven on Earth.

Reversed: Stuck in the past or insecurity.

23. Dagaz -

Meaning: Day

Deities: Ostara or Odin.

Upright: Beginnings, enlightenment, invisibility or

paradox.

Reversed: N/A

Scrying

Scrying involves gazing into a reflective surface to receive visions, insight or messages. You can use a crystal ball, mirror, water, fire a black mirror or other reflective surfaces.

You May…

1. Do this solo or with a group.

2. Choose to ask a specific question for answers.

3. Choose certain lunar phases/solar times to enhance your ability to see.

How to Perform Scrying

Set the tone in a quiet space and relax. Once you're in a calm, meditative state and open to receiving, gaze softly at the surface. Keep your eyes relaxed and unfocused, allowing your vision to slightly blur. Do not look *directly* at the surface but rather within its depths.

Allow visions to appear. Be patient and do not force it. If you do not see anything, that is okay.

If you do see things, you will then interpret them. Pay attention to symbols/images/scenes. Heed any emotions you had. Take note of these, and interpret them based on their personal meanings toward you or by searching their meanings online.

Tasseography

Also known as reading tea leaves/tassology/tasseomancy. This involves interpreting patterns left in a cup by the tea. You can also use coffee grounds or wine sediment. I will be discussing the traditional tea method.

To do this, choose a loose-leaf tea (no bag). People usually use black tea for this. Brew the tea without a strainer so the leaves stay in the cup.

Drink the tea, but leave a small amount (a teaspoon) at the bottom of the cup. Swirl the cup in a circular motion. Place a saucer on top of it and flip the cup over to let the excess liquid drain. Make sure all the liquid is drained before putting the cup upright again. Examine the patterns shown. Common symbols are animals, letters or shapes.

Placement of Symbols

The handle of the cup represents the past or the person asking the question. The bottom represents the present. The rim represents the future.

For advanced tassologists (or if you're feeling up to it) there are cups with different sign inscriptions drawn onto them for further insight.

DIY: Budget Tea Cup

This craft is a good idea for those who are on a budget, not wanting to spend money or anyone who wants to test this out before committing monetarily.

1. Find a white cup with a matching saucer (that no one will care if you write on) or go to the dollar store, thrift store, etc. and get a blank cup and saucer.

2. Get a sharpie. You can use multiple colors, just one color, etc.

3. Draw on the cup and saucer. Some people put the zodiac signs on the saucer, with even lines separating them. They may put planetary sigils and other symbols in the cup, again with lines/spaces separating them.

4. Bake the cup and saucer for 30 minutes at 350 degrees in the oven.

5. Allow them to cool before washing or using.

Also, make sure that the cup is able to withstand that heat based on its material.

Charm Casting

Some people have a collection of charms that they use within other divination readings to provide further messaging and insight. Perhaps you already have a lot of trinkets that you can use. Some people use a mat/cloth with drawn areas such as physical life, love life and more. If they are throwing the charms, the area they land on will denote further meaning. You could also ask a question and pull it one by one.

Bone Throwing

Bone throwing, or osteomancy, can be found across a variety of cultures, such as ancient China, American Hoodoo, Japan, Greece, etc. It is using a set of animal bones and tossing them on the ground/cloth to interpret their positions and orientations. It is similar to charm casting - but with bones. Some Osteomancer add additional items to their throwing kit such as keys, rocks, etc.

You will assign each bone or object a meaning. Some people carve runes into them. Cleanse them before/after reading. Introduce yourself and/or the person you are reading about to the animal spirit and state the issue at hand/question. If the spirit refuses to answer, respect that to avoid angering it.

How to Perform Osteomancy:

To cast, you will gather them in a basket, box or your hands. Next ask your question while shaking them around. Gently toss them onto a cloth or other soft area. Based on where they land, you will be able to interpret them.

With a designed cloth it will be straightforward. If you aren't using one of those, bones that are close to each other can have conjoined meanings. Bones outside of the cloth/area are less important to the answer.

You can choose to read in different directions to represent the past to the future. Items closer to the querent are more urgent/close. Pay attention to a bone that is an outlier. Afterward, some people provide offerings to the animal spirit, especially if it was a long/insightful reading.

Tools Contd.

Athame: A ceremonial dagger used to direct energy, cast circles or invoke protective barriers.

Wand: Utilized to channel and direct magical energy. Used for spell casting, focusing intention and invoking elemental forces.

Chalice: A ritualistic cup used for holding water, wine or other liquids during ceremonies. Symbolic of the water element, it is often used for blessings, libations and communion.

Pentacle: A disc or plate inscribed with a pentagram/other symbols. Representative of the earth element. Used for consecration, charging objects or focal points of rituals.

Cauldron: A large metal pot used for mixing ingredients, burning herbs/incense. Symbolic of transformation and rebirth.

Broom: Symbolic tool used to sweep energy, cleanse spaces and mark boundaries during circle casting.

Bell or Chime: Used to mark the beginning or end of rituals, signal transitions and clear negative energies from a space.

Mirrors: Can be used in scrying, spells, manifestation and more. However, breaking a mirror can be 7 years of bad luck. Some people also believe two mirrors facing each other creates a portal/brings bad luck.

Types of Witches

You do not need to put yourself into a box, although some of you may enjoy it as it pertains to your style of craft. You may check more than one of these. First and foremost, you will generally be coven-based, solitary or hereditary.

I think we all should use as many spiritual tools as we can to manifest our desires, but some may come more naturally than others. For fun, I would consider myself a solitary, cosmic and gray witch. Here are the general types of witches:

Green Witch: Focused on nature, healing and nurturing. Utilizing power, tools and rituals from the earth, greater outdoors, plants, flowers and more.

Hedge Witch: Solely nature. Working alone within their own set rules to develop their own style. Minimalist spells.

Gray Witch: Uses positive and negative spells depending on cause. While some witches are purely positive, the gray witch seeks justice when it's due.

Kitchen Witch: Why is my first thought of Hansel and Gretel? These witches incorporate magic into cooking and baking, they also use a lot of spices found within the kitchen for their work.

Eclectic Witch: One who blends practices from various belief systems together to create their own way of craft.

Sea Witch: You are especially drawn to the ocean, find working and manifesting with it to come with ease. These witches use seawater, seashells etc. in their work.

Cosmic Witch: Those who utilize the power of the Universe. Uses astrology, stellar/lunar magic, divination and is connected with planet Earth's nature.

Black Witch: One who uses magic for dark purposes. Necromancy, binding spells, curses, blood magic or summoning negative entities.

Life Path Numbers

What is your life path number? This is easily discovered online with the wonderful tools at our fingertips. My life path is 11. Let's discover the different numbers and their meanings:

1: The Leader

Independent, ambitious, innovative and determined. Life themes are leadership, self-reliance, and pioneering new ideas. Challenges are that they can be overly assertive, selfish or impatient.

2: The Diplomat

Cooperative, sensitive, diplomatic and peace-loving. Relationships, partnerships and fostering harmony. Can be overly passive, indecisive or avoid conflict.

3: The Communicator

Creative, expressive, sociable and optimistic. Artistic expression, communication and joy. Can be scattered, superficial or prone to mood swings.

4: The Builder

Practical, disciplined, relatable and hardworking. Stability, structure, and building solid foundations. Can be stubborn, rigid or overly cautious.

5: The Adventurer

Freedom-loving, adventurous, adaptable and versatile. Change, exploration and embracing new experiences.

6: The Nurturer

Caring, responsible, nurturing and service-oriented. Family, community and domestic responsibility. Can be overly critical, self-righteous or meddling.

7: The Seeker

Analytical, introspective, spiritual and thoughtful. Inner wisdom, spiritual growth and intellectual pursuits. Can be aloof, skeptical or prone to isolation.

8: The Achiever

Ambitious, authoritative, practical and efficient. Material success, power and achieving goals. Can be materialistic, domineering or aggressive.

9: The Humanitarian

Compassionate, idealistic, selfless and visionary. Global awareness, altruism and humanitarian efforts. Can be naive, impractical or overextended.

11: The Master Intuitive

Visionary, inspirational, intuitive and artistic. Spiritual enlightenment, creativity and intuition. Can be overly sensitive, anxious or self-doubting.

22: The Master Builder

Ambitious, disciplined, practical and visionary. Large-scale achievements, manifesting dreams and practicality. Can be overly-controlling, stressed or fear failure.

33: **The Master Teacher**

Compassionate, nurturing, responsible, and spiritually aware. Teaching, healing and uplifting humanity. Can be overly self-sacrificing, critical and overwhelmed by responsibility.

Angel Numbers

Angel numbers are ways that the Universe (or angels) can communicate with us. When you see these over and over - it could be a sign. Let's go over the fundamental and basic ones:

000: Opportunity

111: Intuition

222: Alignment

333: Support

444: Protection

555: Change

666: Reflection

777: Luck

888: Infinity

999: Release

1010: Personal development

1111: Manifestation

From those you can go forth with what other numbers will mean. However, it is best to still make sure of their definitions. There are so many of them that it would not make sense to write them here. You will find that a lot of explanations will include "divine guidance or support."

Tarot: Everything You Need to Know

When it comes to tarot cards, you really couldn't have picked a better place to learn. I picked up my first deck of tarot cards in Salem, MA, back in 2014. Since then, the cards and I would become inseparable. I have over 10 years of experience specifically with reading tarot and created two original decks, the Specter Cosmos and Gold Tarot. I am more than happy to help you with this form of divination. I am confident I'll be answering any and all questions you have here.

The History of Tarot

Tarot cards were invented in Italy in the 1430s. They were originally called "tarocchi." The earliest decks were hand-painted and used to play card games. They were status symbols - people would commission originally crafted decks.

People began using this tool for divination purposes in the 1780s. A French clergyman, Antoine Court de Gebelin, linked the cards to Egyptian mythology, stating that "tarot" translated to "Royal Road of Life." He was a Protestant pastor as well as a scholar of literature and science. He didn't consider them Satanic/evil but rather a way to gain wisdom. Some people also compared the cards and their symbolism to the Book of Thoth.

Two years later, a French fortune teller, Etteilla (Jean-Baptiste Alliette) would create a book on how to read the cards and make a living off of reading them. He further popularized them with his works and created his own tarot deck where he incorporated astrology and the

four elements.

Tarot Spreads

There seems to be some confusion amongst new readers on how to perform this. Let me start this off by saying that *you do not need to use a spread.* However, it can be nice to avoid the same cards popping out a million times and to get a clear and "bigger picture."

I have been utilizing spreads more lately to get to the point quicker and see the whole story I'm asking about from all angles. There's no specific way to do this. You can even ask the cards a question one by one. You can find many sample spreads on the internet, including Pinterest. You can also use multiple decks in one reading.

How to Pull Cards

There are so many different ways to do this and honestly go with your gut. If you are about to pull a card but your stomach tells you no, and to shuffle once more. You shuffle once more.

You can choose cards by sifting. That is where the deck lays on the palm of one hand while the other runs through each card in an upward pulling motion. Eventually one or more cards will stick out more than the rest.

Another popular way is shuffling the deck with part of the deck in one hand, while the other hand "throws" the cards into the resting hand. You will see this a lot with online tarot readers, so you may know what I'm talking about.

Whether you "knock," utilize incense for cleansing, or shuffle the cards before asking questions is completely up to you. If you are doing readings for someone else, using incense once you go back to your own readings would be advised so that the answers don't get mixed with their energy.

There is no specific way to shuffle tarot cards. Just shuffle them like any regular deck. As long as they are mixed up and randomized, that is what matters.

The Personality of Tarot

Tarot cards have sass. Sometimes they don't want to tell you the whole truth, either. That's when you're asking specific questions you don't know the answer to, and you just keep getting cards like 'The Moon' over and over again.

How to Memorize Them

Practice, practice and practice some more. The booklet that usually comes along with your deck will be your best friend. When you give yourself personal readings and see the results play out in real time, it will make you better. You will understand the cards more, the kinds of circumstances they could be referring to, and so on and so forth.

Tarot Tip

Performing a You vs. Them reading when doing a dynamic between you and someone else. This will teach you what a card would mean for someone else in the future based on your own feelings. Please note that cards do not only mean one thing/emotion and can be liquid depending on situations.

The Zodiac/Time/Astrological Associations

Perhaps you ask the tarot when a situation will occur. Or, it may want to give you an inkling of when a scenario happens. Knowing this information can aid in timeline projection, or putting cards together in a sequence of events. This can also aid in determining who is being referenced (zodiac signs). You can also use the numbers on cards to aid in your timely predictions. To start, here is a general basis of the suit:

Minor Arcana

Wands: Fire signs (Leo, Aries and Saggitarius), Spring, Days and Quick Timing.

Cups: Water signs (Cancer, Scorpio and Pisces), Summer, Months and Mixed Timing.

Swords: Air signs (Aquarius, Gemini and Libra), Autumn, Weeks and Quick Timing.

Pentacles: Earth signs (Taurus, Virgo and Capricorn), Winter, Years and Slow Timing.

Major Arcana, Planets and Deities

The Fool: Uranus/Coelus

The Magician: Mercury/Hermes

The High Priestess: The Moon/Selene

The Lovers: Mercury/Hermes

The Hierophant: Venus/Aphrodite

The Empress: Venus/Aphrodite

The Emperor: Mars/Ares

The Sun: The Sun/Helios

The Hanged Man: Neptune/Poseidon

The Devil: Saturn/Kronos

The World: Saturn/Kronos

Judgment: Pluto/Hades

The Star: Aquarius/Uranus

The Tower: Mars/Ares

The Hermit: Mercury/Hermes

The Chariot: Moon/Selene

Strength: Sun/Helios

Temperance: Jupiter/Zeus

Justice: Venus/Aphrodite

The Moon: Neptune/Poseidon

The Wheel of Fortune: Jupiter/Zeus

Death: Pluto/Hades

Zodiac Signs & Corresponding Major Arcana

Aries: The Emperor

Leo: Strength

Sagittarius: Temperance

Cancer: The Chariot

Scorpio: Death

Pisces: The Moon

Libra: Justice

Aquarius: The Star

Gemini: The Lovers

Capricorn: The Devil

Taurus: The Hierophant

Virgo: The Hermit

There are general tarot card meanings that are good and should be used. But like I said earlier, the more you read and experience life along with their predictions, the more accurately you will be able to construct tangible answers. So, here is what I generally think when I pull certain cards:

The Tower: I never want to see this card again in my life. If I had a choice, I wouldn't! The first time I ever pulled this card, someone got into a near-death car wreck a few days later and has suffered permanent injuries since. Job loss. Break-ups. Things are not working out.

The Empress: Oh yeah, they love me.

Four of Pentacles: Greedy. Said person can only financially support themselves OR they don't want to spend money on anyone but themselves.

The Fool: Making a dumb decision and only being hopeful about it rather than being logical. It could also mean said person is suspended in the air about what to do in a situation.

The Moon: Secrets, not seeing the whole truth. Or the tarot cards are refusing to answer your question because, "You're not supposed to know." *eye roll*.

2 of Cups: So we're official?

3 of Swords: Heartbreak time. Ouch.

3 of Cups: They have lovers on the side, if you know what I mean.

Queen of Swords: The feminine energy has a cutting tongue.

The Chariot: Right side up, moves are being made! Upside down, nothing is happening.

The Magician: Someone is doing spells/manifesting/etc.

The Devil: Purely lust/using someone.

5 of Pentacles: Being left out in the cold (love reading), "Where are we going to live, a shoebox?".

Knight of Cups: An offer!

Five of Swords: Someone is self-sabotaging.

9 of Swords: Being extremely in one's head/stressing out.

Wheel of Fortune: It can go any which way.

Temperance: Balancing emotions.

4 of Cups: Someone is offering a cup of love, but the receiving person would rather look at all the other options (they're not choosing you).

The High Priestess: The feminine's intuition is kicking in.

6 of Swords: Cutting losses and moving on.

Death: It's over. Next!

Auras

Auras can be seen as radiant, pulsing, varying colors surrounding all objects. They come in all different colors. I will say that halos are real but I've only seen one person in my entire life with one.

Essentially, auras are colorful fields of energy surrounding all things. Commonly, people may try to see the auras of themselves or others.

How to See Auras

I recall being in 3rd grade when I asked my friend about the colors she saw surrounding everything when she zoned out. She told me she didn't know what I was talking about. I like to say that "I didn't choose the spiritual life; it chose me." With that being said, I'm happy to say that it came easily to me - and it can to you, too.

In general, you need to sit still and lock your eyes in one spot. Stare at it, be calm. If your eyes unfocus, that is okay. Do not move your eyes. If you are trying to see a person/specific thing's aura, it is best to use a white background to see the true color. Soon, a glow should start to surround the object you're looking at. The longer you look, the more other objects surrounding it will begin to show their colored energy fields until your entire vision is obstructed by aura. Also, some people may have different layers of colors on their auras, which are revealed the longer you stare at them.

You can refer to our 'Colors' section for quick interpretations, or look online for more in-depth meanings of aura colors.

Astrology, Placements and Planetary Magic

This has been my latest delving of work as I completed the Specter Cosmos Tarot (an astrology/mythology/constellation/space deck) last year. I am confident in my knowledge within this sector, but there is always more to learn. Within the following pages, you will find a plethora of knowledge dealing with spells, magic and interpreting the world around you. Let's start with sigils, as much of astrology deals with various symbols.

Sigils

Sigils were historically used to invoke spirits, gods or other supernatural entities. You can use them to focus your intent or manifest your desires. You can use traditional sigils, ones other people have made or make your own. I don't use sigils other people created because I don't know if...

1. It works

2. The meaning they are forecasting is not what they actually charged it as.

To make a sigil, first set your intention clearly. To create the design you can use letters from your statement, subtract the vowels, remove repeated letters and then combine them into a singular design. You can do meditation and allow your hand to move freely to create a drawing unconsciously. You can create a sigil using numerology and put them into a magic square/circle. You can use astrological symbols of planets that represent what you are trying to manifest, etc. After you have created your

design, you can charge it by holding it in your hands and

imagining your energy or a light flowing into it. Other

methods are dancing, chanting or clapping.

To activate it, you can (but are not limited to) burn

it, use blood, use peak emotional states, submerge it in

water, scatter it in the wind or bury it.

Traditional Sigils

Symbols to represent different things within

Esoterica. There are planetary, angel, demon and magical

alphabets that utilize them. Later on I will be touching on

planetary sigils. There are at least 72 angel sigils, 72 demon

sigils, 24 letters in the Theban alphabet and 21 letters in the

Enochian alphabet so I will not be listing them all.

Calculating Charts

To do this, you will need the date, time and place of birth. There are lots of tools online and on websites that will allow you to input this information and receive your chart. There are multiple chart formats, such as Vedic, Tropical, Uranian, Horary, Hellenistic, Sidereal and more. I will be going into the Tropical zodiac below.

Fun fact: Did you know there is a 13th zodiac sign? It is called Ophiuchus the Serpent Bearer, represented by Asclepius the God of Medicine, for those born between November 30th and December 18th.

3,000 years ago, the Babylonians got rid of Ophiuchus and decided 12 was more neat than 13. If we were to add this constellation, many of our signs would be switched! For instance, I would be a Cancer instead of a Leo.

Houses

In astrology there are 12 Houses. Think of these as various categories of life. Some Houses will not have an attributed zodiac sign within your natal (birth) chart. In that case, it denotes that that area of your life won't be influenced in a specific way, or it will not be a central theme. To further interpret an empty House, look at the cusp (closest) planet/sign to it.

First (Ascendant/Rising Sign): House of Self. Ruled by Aries and Mars.

Second: House of Value and Possessions. Ruled by Taurus and Venus.

Third: House of Communication/Sharing. Ruled by Gemini and Mercury.

Fourth (IC): House of Family and Home. Ruled by Cancer and the Moon.

Fifth: House of Pleasure: Ruled by Leo and the Sun.

Sixth: House of Health. Ruled by Virgo and Mercury.

Seventh (Descendant): House of Partnerships. Ruled by Venus and Libra.

Eighth: House of Transformation. Ruled by Scorpio, Mars and Pluto.

Ninth: House of Purpose. Ruled by Sagittarius and Jupiter.

Tenth (MC): House of Social Status. Ruled by Capricorn and Saturn.

Eleventh: House of Friendships. Ruled by Aquarius, Uranus and Saturn.

Twelfth: House of the Subconscious. Ruled by Pisces, Jupiter and Neptune.

The First House is heavily determined by the time you were born. This is because every hour a new sign will be coming up on the eastern horizon, changing your (hence) rising sign. The remaining 2 through 12 signs in each House were in line during the next 11 hours. The zodiac goes in order, starting with Aries and ending with Pisces.

On the other hand, your Descendant sign is directly opposite of the Ascendant on the zodiac wheel. Below you will have a chance to calculate an Ascendant.

Example:

WARNING/DANGER AHEAD: *Math* is utilized in the example below.

Question:

Person A was born at 1:30 pm. Their rising sign (First House) is Taurus. If they were born at the same location on the same day, but at 4:30 pm, what would their rising sign be?

Answer:

Considering Person A was born 3 hours later, we would have to move three Zodiac signs down (in chronological order) from Taurus. Therefore, their rising sign would be Leo.

IC and MC

IC stands for Imum Coeli. Coeli means "sky." Imum means "lowest." The IC is directly opposite of the MC in the zodiac chart wheel.

MC stands for Medium Coeli. Coeli means "sky." Imum means "lowest." MC is also called the Midheaven. It is usually the sign of reaching the highest point in the sky during birth.

North Node and South Node

Again, these two Nodes are on opposing sides of the wheel. The goal is to balance the energies of the two while striving toward the growth of the North Node.

The North Node represents qualities and experiences one is to develop. You are to embrace these qualities within this life. It is associated with personal growth, new opportunities and the future.

As for the South Node, it signifies qualities, behaviors and experiences that are comfortable and familiar. It can be linked to similar living styles of your past life or early life experiences. It can indicate innate abilities or tendencies.

If one overly-relies on their South Node it can lead to stagnation. People may avoid their North Node opportunities to continue on the path of their South.

In relation to the assigned planets and zodiac signs, you will note that your own chart likely won't match what is listed in the Houses above.

Part of Fortune

Part of Fortune, or Fortuna, represents luck, success and prosperity. It is used to indicate areas of life where one will find joy, achievement and fulfillment. It can also represent where material and emotional prosperity is found. Your innate talents and abilities are highlighted with this position.

Fortuna is calculated in two ways. For those born during the day, you will add the Ascendant and Moon sign together and subtract the Sun sign. For people born during the night, you will add the Ascendant and Sun sign together and subtract the Moon sign.

The House in which the Part of Fortune resides shows the area of life you can expect the most success and well-being. The zodiac sign shows what qualities will aid you in harnessing your success. Aspects (multiple planets) can enhance or hinder its influence.

Major Aspects

Aspects are angular relationships between planets, points or other celestial bodies in a chart. There are Major and Minor Aspects. They reveal the dynamics between energies. Get ready to do geometry!

Conjunctions (0° to 10°)

Conjunctions are when two or more planets align via sign or degree within one's natal chart. Planets should be within 10° of each other to be considered a conjunction. The closer together, the more influential.

With this said, a person will be influenced by both planets in a blended way. If the planets in conjunction go well together, it can have a positive effect and vice versa. The houses each planet is in will play an important factor as well.

Opposition (180°)

Opposition means what it sounds like, opposing sides. This is when two planets are directly on opposite sides of each other. This creates tension and balance, resulting in a need for compromise or confrontation.

Square (90°)

When do planets are at a 90° angle from each other. This signifies obstacles and or conflict that require action to solve.

Trine (120°)

When two planets are 120° apart. The nature of this aspect is harmonious and supportive. This shows an ease of flow between planetary energies.

Sextile (60°)

Two planets 60° apart from each other. This is a positive and cooperative aspect. It tells of opportunities and communication being at ease between planetary influences.

Major Aspect Symbols

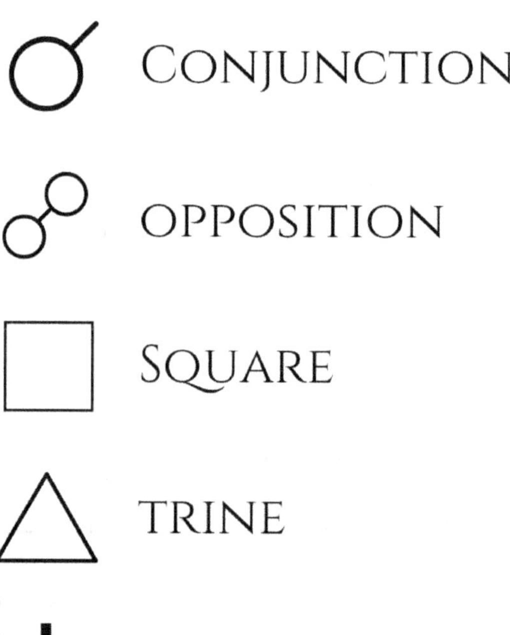

Minor Aspects

Minor Aspects are less pronounced degree separations. As they are Minor, they are meant to be translated as affecting people in less potent ways as to Major.

Additionally, there are such things as Orbs, which denotes the proximity of two planets. The further apart, the less intense, and vice versa. Also, planetary strength should be considered based on each planet's inherent qualities. Values are numerical, either positive or negative. Negative values suggest challenges/stress and vice versa.

Quincunx (150°)

Quincunx is a 150° distance between two planets. It shows a need for adjustment or adaptation. It indicates areas of one's life that require balance and integration.

Semisquare (45°)

45° variance. Mild tensions and irritations to be addressed. Not as intense as a square.

Sesquiquadrate (135°)

135° degrees apart between two planets. Similar to the Semisquare. Indicates mild tensions and adjustments that need to be made.

Semisextile (30°)

30° distance between two planets. A subtle potential for smaller opportunities and challenges. It serves to show areas of one's life where they can develop a new skill or understanding.

Quintile (72°)

72° distance between two planets. Associated with creative expressions, talent and innovation. This can show a natural aptitude for particular skills and talents.

Biquintile (144°)

144° distance between two planets. Essentially double Quintile. This is considered a harmonious aspect. It enhances creativity and originality. It can lead to breakthroughs or unconventional approaches. It can allow individuals to see things from other perspectives.

Minor Aspect Symbols

 QUINCUNX

 SEMISQUARE

 SESQUIQUADRATE

 SEMISEXTILE

Q QUINTILE

bQ BIQUINTILE

Remaining Celestial Sigils

What are these? Remember in the "sigils" section, I briefed the planetary ones. Like the tarot, I urge you to memorize them so you can read them quickly. I promise it is so much easier to look at it and instantly know what it means rather than fighting it.

There are sigils from the Sun to Pluto. Additionally, you will find the North and South Nodes, Lilith, Chiron, Ceres, Vertex, Eris, Midheaven, Pallas, Vesta, Part of Fortune, Transpluto, Pallas, Juno, Ascendant and Nessus.

Planet Sigils & More

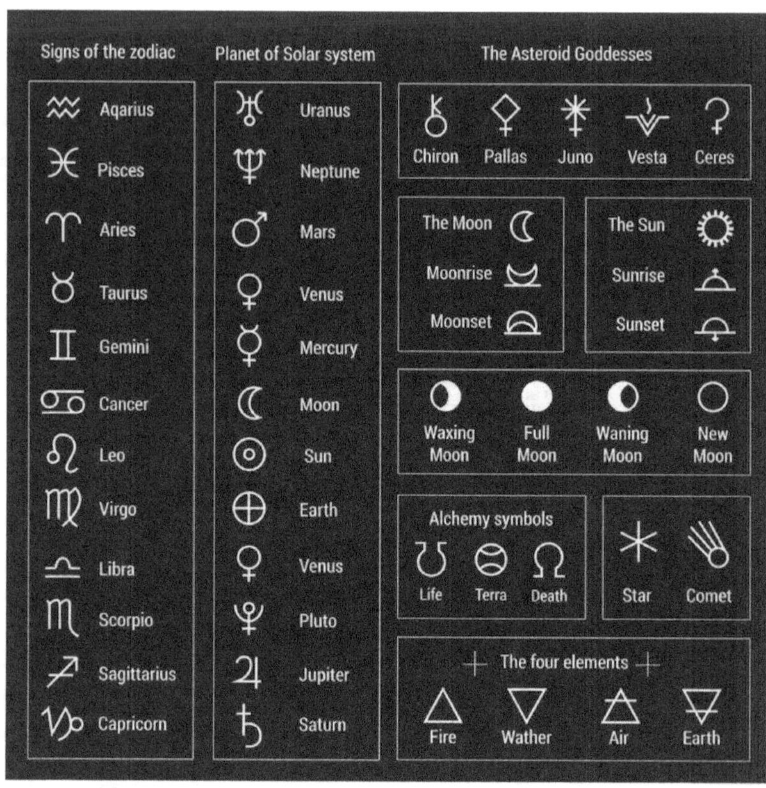

Other Signifiers

There are other calculations found within the chart. These are based on the number of signs per placement. For instance, natal charts commonly show how many signs one has of Fire, Water, Air or Earth. Using this you can see the overall common elemental energies. Also, it shows the amount of Masculine vs. Feminine signs found.

Cardinal, Fixed and Mutable signs are also noted. Each category has one of each element in it.

Cardinal signs are the first sign at the start of a new season. Therefore, they're about innovation and trying new things. Leadership, being proactive and drive to start new ventures are key components of them.

Fixed signs are dedicated to maintaining, upholding and defending their positions every day. They are the least welcoming of change. They preserve tradition. These signs embody their season fully.

Mutable signs are placed at the end of seasons. They are adaptable to change and differing circumstances. Seen as versatile and open-minded. They are good at going with the flow.

Cardinal: Aries, Cancer, Libra and Capricorn.

Fixed: Taurus, Leo, Scorpio and Aquarius.

Mutable: Gemini, Virgo, Sagittarius and Pisces.

Dreams

Dreams do have meaning. It is a way for your subconscious mind to speak to you. You may have noticed in the past, when stressed, you could have had nightmares. It was for a reason, your brain knew how you felt.

The brain is an interesting thing. It translates the world around us into a perceptible movie. It creates lifelike dreams out of nothing.

Dreams are very symbolic as well. Whenever I am extremely stressed, I usually have dreams of dying. One time I was very stressed about a career move and had a nightmare that my head was clean-cut through my neck, but was still balancing on it as I waited for it to inevitably fall off. My dream didn't let me die and I remained that way until I woke up. True story but dreams are crazy; we all know this.

If you would like, you can use a dream journal to keep track. Pay attention to common/recurring themes.

Analyze symbolism, as well as other things that could have meaning to you. Utilize context from your real life. How did you feel during the dream? Take note of your emotions.

Different analysis styles you can use are Freudian, Jungian and modern psychological analysis. Freudian is to focus on your unconscious desires and conflicts. Jungian is to interpret archetypes and the collective unconscious. As for modern psychological analysis, you would consider them as a daily way to process emotions and experiences.

Frequencies

Frequencies are fun, easy and relaxing ways to add power to your spells or manifestations. Different Hz will have different attraction properties. I like using 888 Hz for money and abundance.

Once you find a frequency that aligns with your intentions, you can play a video on YouTube that has it. You can play it in the background during spell casting. You can play it on low volume when you sleep. You can even use it during meditation.

Meditation

Meditation is a way of calming one's mind to be clear of thought and focus on being present. To do this, find a quiet space, sit down and get comfortable. You are to keep your back straight and place your hands in your lap on your knees.

To start, you can begin with just 5-10 minutes of meditation. If you enjoy this practice you can continue on and lengthen the duration. Optionally, you can set the mood with incense and calming background music. Close your eyes and take a few deep breaths to relax.

Types of Meditation

Mindfulness: Allowing thoughts to come, acknowledging them and letting them pass.

Body Scan: Awareness of one's body from head to toe, in search of any sensations.

Guided: A pre-recorded guided meditation or in-person.

Mantra: To repeat a sound to help one focus during meditation.

Visualization: Imagining a peaceful scene.

Chakras

Within your energy field, there is believed to be 7 chakras of different colors. They are believed to be responsible for one's confidence and self-esteem to feel in control of their life. People work to clear and balance their chakras/energy flow which can be blocked. People use meditation, yoga, sound, affirmations and reconnecting with nature as a way to unblock them. From bottom to top they are:

1. Root; red. Stability and comfort.

2. Sacral; orange. Sexuality and pleasure.

3. Solar Plexus; yellow. Power and strength.

4. Heart; green. Compassion and kindness.

5. Throat; blue. Communication.

6. Third Eye; indigo. Imagination and intuition.

7. Crown Chakra; purple. Spiritual connection.

Spellcasting Basics

Now that you have a solid spiritual understanding, let's put that knowledge to use. It doesn't do anything just sitting in your head. Before you begin partaking in spells to manifest new beginnings or desires, I highly suggest you partake in a deep cleanse. The truth is - you can manifest love, finances, etc. all you want - but if there is a curse or hex placed on you, you won't receive it.

Witching Hours: Times and Days

Times

12 am: Spells for banishing, protection, psychic work and contacting spirits. Veil between worlds is the thinnest.

1 - 2 am: Introspection, deep meditation and spiritual insight.

3 - 4 am: The "Witching Hour". A potent time for transformative magic, astral travel and dream work.

5 - 6 am: New beginnings, purification, renewal and intention setting.

7 - 8 am: Clarity, focus, communication and planning.

9 - 10 am: Productivity, success, empowerment and career advancement.

11 am - 12 pm: Power and manifestation. Spells for ambition, influence, confidence and personal goals.

1 - 2 pm: Leadership, authority, recognition and public speaking.

3 - 4 pm: Enhance creativity, artistic endeavors, innovation and problem-solving.

5 - 6 pm: Abundance, prosperity, wealth and finance.

7 -8 pm: Love spells, relationship harmony, emotional healing and nurturing connections.

9 - 10 pm: Relaxation, inner peace, dream magic and subconscious healing.

11 am - 12 am: Banishing, protection and spell work.

Days

Sunday: Success, vitality, leadership, health and spiritual growth spells. Day of the Sun.

Monday: Emotions, intuition, psychic abilities, fertility and feminine energy. Day of the Moon.

Tuesday: Courage, protection, strength, conflict resolution and overcoming obstacles. Day of Mars.

Wednesday: Communication, wisdom, knowledge, education, divination and creativity. Day of Mercury.

Thursday: Abundance, prosperity, luck, expansion and spiritual growth. Day of Jupiter.

Friday: Love, romance, beauty, friendship, harmony and creativity. Day of Venus.

Saturday: Grounding, protection, boundaries, discipline, wisdom and banishing negativity. Day of Saturn.

Basic Lunar Magic

The Moon goes through cycles of waxing and waning (coming and going). The Moon is commonly associated with the (water) star sign Cancer (the crab).

Moon Phases

During the Full Moon phase it is an optimal time to practice witchcraft or watch your spellwork from two weeks prior come to fruition. Different star signs can be featured, which may sway what spellwork you perform or how well certain manifestations occur. It is also a good time to practice gratitude and recharge crystals in the moonlight. Moon water can be created by placing a clear jar of water in the moonlight as well.

Waxing Moon Phases (the phases leading up to the full moon) are great for spells focusing on expansion or growth. Waning Moon Phases (after the full moon) are great for banishing, cutting cords or releasing spellwork.

You can utilize the time of a New Moon (moon is invisible)

to imbue a fresh start or face our shadow selves. And so,

the cycle continues!

Moon Phase Graphic

Waxing (left) to Waning (right.)

General Don'ts

Isn't it nice when someone informs you of what *not* to do so you don't make the same mistake? You may not all listen, but I figured I'd at least warn you. Within this sector you will find general guidelines within the spiritual community for a variety of spellwork.

1. When working with deities, do not show disrespect.

2. When doing an *egg cleanse* (you will read about this later on), do not look directly over top of the egg.

3. Do not watch the egg when you dispose of it during an egg cleanse.

4. Do not step or dance in a fairy circle. (I had a friend who accidentally did this and was haunted by nightmares with the faye, etc.)

5. Do not mess with fairies. Just as a general guideline. Don't go in their fairy circle. Don't dance in it. Don't take any of the stuff from their area; don't give them iron; be weary of time; and don't underestimate them.

6. Some witches believe in the "rule of three" which states that anything you put out will be sent back to you threefold. Therefore, a lot of them may not practice black magic due to that.

7. Being disrespectful toward the free will of others. This one is up for debate and depends on your personal moral compass.

8. Don't try to bind dragons.

9. When working with spirits, protect yourself and clearly define boundaries.

10. Angels are not as easy to work with as you think and can be aloof when it comes to human emotion. They are warriors and messengers of God; remember that.

11. Protect yourself when working with demons. They can be dangerous and manipulative. Before you try ANY demon work you need to do extensive research.

12. Never doing protection work.

When in doubt, search about. As an additional disclaimer, I want to let everyone know that within the world of spirituality there are a lot of nuances that may not be told to you at first. For instance, within the community there is a lot of speculation about who can practice what kind of craft. For instance, voodoo and hoodoo practitioners like to keep their beliefs within their group of people and can get offended if someone outside of their lineage uses them. I am unsure of the complexities of all the different religions - because I just stick to my own - but since this is a general grimoire, we will be glossing over everything. It is up to you to do your research and decide if it is a fit, like I have been reiterating.

Briefly within this section I will name every form and style of witchcraft. With this you will be able to research each one and see if it fits you based on heritage, ease, etc.

Voodoo (West African/Haitian/Caribbean)

Hoodoo (African American)

Wicca

Traditional Witchcraft

Santería (Cuban)

Druidry (Ancient Celtic)

Chaos Magic

Ceremonial Magic

Thelema

Shamanic Witchcraft

Modern Satanism

Elemental

Necromancy

Alchemy

Pagan

Sufi

Taoist Magic

Neo-Paganism

Folk

Vedic (India)

Huna (Native Hawaiian)

Sumerian (Ancient Mesopotamia)

Celtic

Buddhist Witchcraft

Norse Heathenry

Roman Witchcraft

Egyptian Witchcraft

Hellenistic Witchcraft (Greek)

Spells

Finally it is time to learn and try some spells. In this section I will give you three spells per category. The categories are Hex/Curse Removal, Protection, Love, Binding and Money. This is a good way to get you going with tried and true methods.

Hex/Curse Removal

Step One: Diagnostic Testing

Before you take a nose dive into ridding yourself of negative occurrences, check to see if you've experienced symptoms listed below. After you determine that you could be cursed/hexed, I suggest starting with an egg cleanse.

- Infestations.

- Inability to find work/get a job/job loss.

- Random bad things happening one after another.

- Illness/chronic illness.

- Fatigue/brain-fog.

- Nightmares.

- Negative energy.

- Disturbed relationships.

- Negative paranormal activity.

- Fearfulness and or anxiety.

- Personal items disappearing/moving.

- Intuitive feelings about being hexed/cursed.

Egg Cleanse

Purpose: The egg cleanse is used to get rid of negative energy or forces attached or put upon you.

Ingredients:

- 1 egg

- 1 bowl

Instructions:

1. Hold the egg in your hands and concentrate on your intention.

2. Visualize any negative energy or influences transferring to the egg while you rub it on yourself starting from head to toe.

3. *Do not look at this from the top, only the side* Crack the egg into a glass of water and wait five minutes.

4. Examine the egg *from the side of the glass* and yolk in the water. Read the patterns and shapes

formed by the egg to gain insight into the nature of the negativity.

5. Optional: to return negative energy to sender, add chili pepper, cayenne pepper, red pepper flakes or hot sauce and salt.

6. Add salt to it before flushing it down the toilet. Do not look at it while you flush it.

7. Afterwards, perform cleansing via incense, sage, etc.

Potential Interpretations:

Bubbles: Energy being released.

White, cloudy bubbles: Health issues.

Bubbles on the yolk: Surrounded by people who love and support you.

Foam: Something unknown in the background.

Clear: No negativity.

Cobwebs: Daily negativity picked up from every day.

Yolk does not sink: Negative energy was sent to you intentionally by someone else.

Discoloration: You are fearful of something.

Large o's: Something is holding you down.

Double yolk: Pregnancy.

Spirals/spikes: Negative energy hanging over your head.

Blood: Needing to heal.

Uncrossing Ritual

Purpose: To remove negative influences, blockages or curses affecting you.

Ingredients:

- A black candle

- Sea salt or salt.

- A bowl of water.

- Incense.

- A mirror (optional.)

- A cauldron.

- A white candle.

- Herbs such as rue, basil or bay leaf.

Instructions:

1. Clearly set your intent to remove or resolve any blockages, curses or negative influences.

2. Cleanse the area you are performing the ritual in. Make sure it is physically clean and clutter-free.

3. Light your incense to spiritually cleanse the area.

4. Cast a circle.

5. Light the black candle, placed on the left, to represent the removal of negativity.

6. Light the white candle, placed to the right, to represent purification and positive change.

7. State your intentions out loud. Focus your energy on the removal of these blockages.

8. Sprinkle salt around the space or on the floor of work. Burn the uncrossing herbs in a heatproof dish or cauldron. Let the smoke cleanse the space.

9. (Optional) Hold a mirror in front of you and visualize all negative influences being reflected away from you and back from whence they came.

10. Dip your fingers into the bowl of water, sprinkle some on yourself, or wash your hands or face with it. Visualize the water washing away the negative energy.

11. As you perform your cleanse, continue to affirm the intention for purity and freedom.

12. Extinguish the black candle, then the white. Visualize the negative energy being completely dissolved and replaced with positive and healing energy.

13. Dispose of any ashes and salt. You may bury them or throw them away. Do not leave them in your home.

Timing Suggestions

For maximum efficiency, perform this during a waxing moon for growth and removal, or during a full moon for maximum effectiveness.

Bath Cleanse

I created this one on my own and it worked. You can call it a "lazy uncrossing ritual variation." You just need a bathtub and water. You can add different herbs/essential oils to it if you wish, but my water had nothing in it.

Get in the tub and get into a relaxed state. State that you are getting rid of all negative energy, evil eyes, hexes, curses - anything under the Sun sent your way that is negatively affecting you - with this bath water. You are cleansing yourself. Make sure every part of your body is submerged at some point. No Achilles heels! You may also rub your arms, legs, etc. as if you are "cleansing" the influences off of you.

State that all the negative energy is now in the bath water and will not reconnect with you. Before you drain the water, state that it will now leave you to never return or affect you again. Drain the water. As you stand up, again state that none of the negative energy in the water will stick

with you or affect you.

You're done! It's very similar to a baptism.

Protection Spells

Perhaps you just completed your hex and curse removals. Congratulations! So…are you just going to stand there with nothing to protect you when someone else places another spiritual attack on you?

You never truly know what other people are up to or their intentions. You can *never* be *too* safe. With that being said, let's dive into how you can protect yourself from the evil eye, curses, hexes, bad energy and more.

Protection Crystal Spell

Purpose: To absorb negative energies that may come your way and reflect them back onto the sender.

Ingredients:

- 1 protection crystal (black tourmaline/obsidian, labradorite, selenite, etc.)

Instructions:

1. Cleanse your crystal to dispel prior energies or attributions from it.

2. Clear your head and focus.

3. Hold your crystal in between both of your closed hands.

4. Get clear on what the crystal will do energetically and speak the intentions out loud. Example: "This crystal will serve as a protection against any and all negative influences placed intentionally or unintentionally upon me, my life and my surroundings." Go into as much depth as you wish.

5. Feel your energy flowing into the rock as you speak your intentions.

6. When you're done, say "mote it be."

7. Keep the stone with you.

Protection & New Opportunities Spell

Purpose: Protection and riddance of hexes.

Ingredients:

- 432 Hz.

- Incense.

- A white candle.

- Black tourmaline.

Instructions:

1. Turn on 432 Hz background sound.

2. Light incense and clear the room of prior energies, and utilize it to clear any current negative attachments as well.

3. Light the white candle.

4. Rub the black tourmaline stone all over your body from head to toe, imagining it taking away all negative energy, evil eyes, etc.

5. Chant, "By candle's light, this spell is spun. Protection and prosperity, now begun. Negative

energies fade away. New opportunities, come my

way," at least three times.

6. Once complete, say "mote it be."

Temporary Protection Jewelry Spell

Purpose: To solely provide protection. Good for wire-wrapped crystals on a necklace or jewelry to be enchanted.

Ingredients:

- 1 white candle.

- Amethyst/jewelry piece.

- Sage.

- Black candles.

Instructions:

1. Wash and cleanse the amethyst.

2. Carve the sigil of Ingwaz into the white candle.

3. Light the sage and black candles.

4. Light the white candle.

5. Charge the amethyst/jewelry with the intention of it providing protection.

6. Wear the stone or jewelry whenever you are wanting protection.

Self-Reflection Spell

For this you will need a closable, double sided compact mirror, pencil and paper. It is straight-forward and simple.

On a piece of paper, write the full name of the person and their date of birth.

Optional step: Add herbs to the center of the piece of paper. You can do healing herbs if you want them to heal, pepper if you want it to hurt/pack a punch, etc.

Fold the piece of paper away from yourself and place it in the mirror. Close the mirror. Bind it with your material of choice (wrapping string-like material around it and tying) and bury it or put it in your freezer.

You may unbury, take it out of the freezer etc. once you believe they have had enough time to reflect.

Bring Us Together Love Spell

Purpose: This spell is used to bind two people together.

Ingredients:

- 2 red stick candles.

- A lighter.

- A piece of paper.

- Rose petals.

- Rose and Lavender essential oils.

- Salt/incense.

- A fireproof dish.

- A red pen.

- Pouch/cloth bag.

- A long thread of some kind (preferably red.).

Instructions:

1. Cleanse your space with either salt or incense.

2. Cast a protective circle.

3. Inscribe one person's first and last name as well as their date of birth per candle.

4. Anoint the red candles with essential oil while focusing on your intentions.

5. Place the candles within proximity of one another.

6. Light the candles and imagine your intentions coming to fruition.

7. Write each person's name on the piece of paper.

8. Wrap the thread around the piece of paper to bind. During this time, chant "With this knot I bind our love, strong and true as stars above, By the power of fire, water, earth and air, our hearts are joined, a perfect pair."

9. Sprinkle rose petals around the bound parchment paper. Place the paper and petals into a small pouch or cloth bag.

10. Drip a few drops of wax from both of the red candles onto the pouch to seal your intentions.

11. Allow the candles to burn out completely while focusing on your desires.

12. Place the pouch somewhere it will not be disturbed.

13. Thank any spiritual entities or guides that assisted

you.

14. Close your protective circle.

Attraction Spell

Purpose: This spell is used to attract a person back to the other.

Ingredients:

- 2 red stick candles.

- 1 pink candle.

- A lighter.

- 2 red candles.

- Rose, lavender and vanilla essential oils.

- Spell jar.

- Honey or sugar.

- Bay leaf/leaves.

- Pink paper or pink sticky note.

- Pen.

Instructions:

1. Visualize how you want the other person to act and speak from their perspective.

2. Light the 2 red candle sticks, each representing one person.

3. Anoint the candle with rose, lavender and vanilla essential oil.

4. Add more essential oils to the candle that symbolizes the person who is to be attracted to the other.

5. Scatter crushed bay leaves amongst them to symbolize generosity and spending money on the other person.

6. Optional: Add sugar or honey to the altar for sweetness.

7. Write from their POV on a pink sticky note or pink piece of paper. Sign the end of the note with their name. Be sure they mention your first and last name in the note.

8. Add essential oils onto the note.

9. Fold the paper three times toward you.

10. Put spell remnants/scattered ingredients into the spell jar.

11. Roll the folded note toward you to fit into the jar, and place it inside.

12. Put on the spell jar's cork and seal it with their stick candle's wax.

13. Once solidified, place the jar underneath your bed and sleep.

Can also light an orange candle for faster results.

Notes: Make sure their candle burns all the way down first.

Money Spells

Money and Luck Spell

Purpose: Best performed on the evening of a new moon.

Ingredients:

- A green candle.

- Cinnamon powder.

- Purse or old wallet.

- 3 coins.

- A spoon.

- A bowl.

- Pine oil.

- Ground nutmeg.

Instructions:

1. Cleanse your space and gather your ingredients.

2. Anoint the green candle with pine oil and light it.

3. Put nutmeg and cinnamon in the bowl and mix the ingredients with the spoon.

4. Be specific on the amount of money you want to receive and imagine it coming into your possession.

5. Focus on the amount of money as you toss the 3 coins. Continue to toss the coins until you get one tail and two heads.

6. Put the coins in the wallet or purse and shake it while doing a money chant.

7. Put the purse or wallet in the same place as your financial documents are and leave it there.

Money Attraction Bay Leaf

Purpose: To easily attract money and finances to the subject.

Ingredients:

- Your wallet.

- A bay leaf.

Instructions:

1. Grab your ingredients.

2. Get a bay leaf.

3. Speak the intention to the leaf while holding it in your hands. Consciously charge it with the duty of attracting wealth.

4. Place the bay leaf in your wallet and keep it there.

Money Spell

Purpose: To bring in finances.

Ingredients:

- Coins.

- Cinnamon.

- Rice.

- A plate.

- A green stick candle.

- 8 bay leaves.

- 8 cloves.

- Yarn.

- Oil (olive oil, etc.)

Instructions:

1. Wrap the green candle with 8 bay leaves, 8 cloves - fastening them to the stick with a piece of yarn wrapping around it 8 times.

2. Pour rice on the plate and make a circle. Add cinnamon.

3. Place a coin in the middle of the rice circle and

place the candle on top of it.

4. Douse the candle in your choice of oil.

5. Light the candle and let it burn completely.

6. Never use the coin again.

Deity Work: A Preface

Even as a seasoned practitioner myself, there are certain deities and spiritual practices I personally stay away from. Mostly because there is SO much false information on the internet that I do not trust. I believe I could do it if I had the correct instructions.

For instance, I have never tried working with Hecate or angels. Why? Because I *know* that if you do it wrong it could be really bad. I also understand that while they are extremely powerful I am not at the point where I want to work with them unless they reach out to me.

There are easier deities to work with and I recommend that you start with the more forgiving, easy-going ones. I actually beg you to if you're new to this. I'm saving you.

You should be scared. You should be weary. You should feel like you're tip-toeing at first. In fact, I don't think being super macho toward a powerful spiritual being is ever a good idea. Unless you're working with evil ones, then I'd suggest having confidence so that you don't get taken advantage of.

Many of you will probably have grown up with a religion. I was raised as a Christian.

Insert weird experience here

When I was young, I had to be in third grade or earlier, I was reading the Bible. I know I was really into it at one point and brought it to school to read and my teacher told me I couldn't bring it to school. I'm not a Christian anymore but I still feel like that was a little messed up but I guess that is the rule in America and I have to respect it!

I was reading the Bible at home, specifically Revelation, which interested me and so many others. The strangest part was I saw it say something along the lines of,

"...but one day, Satan will rise again and take over the World."

I can honestly tell you that is not what I read word for word but I can't remember the exact sentence from 15 plus years ago. It's a miracle I even remember that honestly.

I remember my heart rate increasing and I immediately stopped reading the book and ran to my parents to show them. When I tried to show them, it was no longer written. *As a disclaimer, I am not dyslexic.*

Do I think God and Jesus are real? Perhaps, but not the teachings that have been construed by various Kings/Queens to fit their agendas, editing/deleting parts of the Bible, humans who have written it with inevitable bias, etc. I think for anyone to say,

"My religion is one hundred percent true. Source? Just trust me." Is crazy. Even with all of the stuff I am teaching you here; there is no way a human mind can accurately conceptualize the other side with complete accuracy. There will be errors.

We also are so involved with everyday life that we forget - we are smaller than a speck of dust when compared to the size of the Universe. Space does not revolve around us. This can be scary but I think it should be freeing you of stress and worries.

At the end of the day, no matter what legacy you leave, no matter how you live your life - eventually the Earth and its inhabitants will cease to exist, forget your name and the Universe will go on. One thing that holds true is that energy cannot be created nor destroyed. So while *you* may not be here, the energy you hold will forever be a part of the Universe, transferred to different forms for eternity.

<u>Fun fact</u>: Did you know that humans are made from stars? Yes, you are a child of a star. How beautiful is that? I wonder which form your energy will take on next.

As for the afterlife there is no certain way to determine this. Even with near-death experiences from people across the world, we must remember that when you

die your brain emits DMT, or Dimethyltryptamine, when

you die. So those tales could be of a DMT experience.

Deity Work

There are seemingly endless deities one can work with. Who you choose to have relations with is up to your discernment. I believe it is a matter of finding who works best with you, trial and error.

I think it is also important to not rely all of your energy on them because they still have free will. They don't *have* to do anything. In order to increase your chances of getting your wishes granted, do your research on them/what they like for offerings and how you would approach them. Avoid being disrespectful.

A Few of My Experiences

In my time of practice I have worked with Lakshmi, Aphrodite, Loki, Hades and Plouton. I will describe my general experiences with each.

I have found Aphrodite to not give me what I want in love, but what I need. With that said - do not work with her if you are wanting a toxic relationship to stay together because that is not what she does.

I worked with Lakshmi for beauty and money. She never gave me consistent income but I did get a lump sum of money per each interaction we had. In terms of beauty, I did not get more beautiful but the *glamour* and rose-colored glasses were turned up for me and everyone around me in regards to my appearance.

Hades is tricky - he is actually known to be a trickster. I am not sure how to feel about it. The first time I worked with him, as seen below, it went very well. But since then I feel he has teased me in terms of results by showing me what I asked for and then ripping it away at the

last second. Or giving me a check for three cents when I

asked for money, no joke. I have since refrained from

dealing with him.

Loki I have enjoyed working with. I have provided

a simple deal I do with him on the second to find lost items.

The craziest part is that it works every time within a span of

5 seconds of asking.

In lieu of Loki, I recall one time I had lost my car

keys for two weeks, my family and I turned the house

upside down looking for them. I told them, "I give up, I'm

asking Loki where to find it," and they laughed at me and

told me to do whatever works. They saw me ask in the

kitchen. Within five seconds an image of a pocket in my

Mom's car flashed like an image in my mind.

It was in that spot. I went to my parent's room

where they were lying and held the keys up in the air. I told

them where it was, and they explained that it was

impossible because we already checked there. They were visibly in shock and a little freaked out. That was the first time I did it.

Ploutos is a blind and lame God due Zeus. He is commonly mistaken with Hades (Pluto/Plouton/Pluton) and is the bestower of wealth, but due to his disabilities he does not distribute it only amongst the good. He takes time to come to you. So, do not work with him if you need money pronto.

Before Working With a Deity

Do your research to find a deity that aligns with what your goals are. Be sure to read up on their mythology, personality, symbolism and more.

Be respectful, it never hurts to be kind. You may provide offerings that they prefer, found from your research. You may communicate with them via prayer, ritual or meditation. Clearly state your intentions, requests or gratitude. At the end of the day, deities have their own will and may choose not to grant requests.

Example No. 1

Deity: Hades

Offering:

- Coins

- Honey

- Olive oil

- Water

Candle:

- Green

Asked for:

Money (Higher paying jobs, specifically).

Result:

This worked for me, even though it took 4 months to come to fruition.

Example No. 2

Deity: Loki

Offering:

- Candy

Asked for:

Loki to tell me where my lost item is in return for a piece of candy.

Result:

This works for me every time like a charm.

Manifestation

Manifestation can be compared to Quantum Jumping, which will be discussed in the next section. You may have heard of the Law of Attraction - this is what manifesting is. If you have not already, I suggest you watch the movie 'The Secret' and it will explain this perfectly!

Essentially, the Law of Attraction is the belief that positive and negative thinking can influence your life. It states that you can utilize it to bring your dream life to fruition. The principles are (in simple terms) to ask (and get clear on what you want), to believe, to trust and receive.

Techniques

As for techniques for manifestation, people commonly also use positive thinking, meditation, practicing gratitude and aligning themselves emotionally to enhance the ability to capture their desires. You can use positive affirmations starting with, "I am." You may also act as if you already have everything you want.

I personally use visualization the most. I enjoy creating vision boards as well, which falls underneath that category. Essentially you will gather images, words, sayings and more of what you want to bring into your life. You can make this digitally or print out pictures to put on a physical board.

Manifestation Key No. 1

I need it, I need it, I want it…

Stop. Thinking. About. It.

"But won't my manifestation not arrive if I don't think long and hard about it?" You may ask. Let me put it this way - have you ever thought of someone and forgot about it and then they text you or you see them in public? That's how quick you can manifest if you let it go.

That is the key - letting go and letting the Universe. It's almost like when you are in kahoots with someone - the more you want them the less they want you. Make sense?

Manifestation Key No. 2

Now that you are so excited to start this new life, you might be wanting to tell all of your friends. However, I suggest against this. I will be going in depth about this in 'Quantum Jumping' but for now just *don't do it*.

A Personal Experience

I've been practicing these methods since 2014. I have successfully brought a lot of blessings into my life with it. I recall once, I put on my vision board that I wanted to go to a Blackbear concert. My first semester in college, Blackbear played and I got to go for free because I was a student. Awesome, right?

Quantum Jumping

To put it simply - Quantum Jumping is manifestation on steroids. To understand Quantum Jumping I want you to understand Quantum Mechanics and Quantum Theory. Welcome to Jessica Specter's crash course, The No-Math-Involved-Because-Math-is-the-Devil, Simplified Explanation of Woo-Woo Science for Artistically Inclined Right Brain Thinkers.

Put simply, Quantum Theories is *literally* magic and manifestation for everyone who isn't witchy. People will say, "magic isn't real," and call you dumb for believing/practicing it when this literally exists and has been proven. Who's laughing now? There are even uncovered CIA documents on this subject.

Quantum Jumping is essentially where one moves into a different timeline or shifts into a new reality. In Quantum Theory, there are multiple Universes all occurring at the same time ((time does not exist it is a human construct) that is a solid fact). Therefore, all lifestyles, experiences etc. can and have already occurred. To learn more about this, I have an in-depth video uploaded to my YouTube channel. View the 'Connect' section to find it.

Bonus: For those of you who are interested, there is also something called astral projection where you leave your body during sleep to travel the world around you and interact with other worldly beings. Supposedly, you are attached to your body via a spiritual umbilical cord while doing this. I am not speaking on this because <u>I have never done it</u>, therefore I don't think I'm qualified to. But I still wanted to mention this to you so you can do your own research and try it.

A Final Word

With that, you are officially on your way to cultivating the life of your dreams and bending reality. I truly hope you learned a lot, or for the seasoned practitioners a handful of new information. I hope this book serves as a daily reference and guide.

If you enjoyed this grimoire or found it useful, I ask that you leave an honest review on GoodReads and/or the platform in which you purchased your copy. All feedback is greatly appreciated. I am sending love your way.

Xoxo,

Jessica Specter

Connect

For all of my updated links, visit my Linktree.

Linktree: https://linktr.ee/jessicaspecter

Instagram: @jessicaspecterdsgn

YouTube: @jessicaxspecter

FaceBook: @jessicaspecterdsgn

TikTok: @jessicaxspecter

Author Biography

Jessica Specter has been a dedicated practitioner of tarot and various mystical crafts for over a decade. She is the creator of two original tarot decks, the Specter Gold and the Cosmos Tarot. For much of her journey, Jessica kept her spiritual practices private, only recently sharing her experiences and insight with the world.

In addition to her work in the mystical arts, Jessica is a versatile author. Her literary repertoire includes the 'Specter Thriller Collection' and the charming children's book 'All About Bears.' She received a Bachelor's degree in Communication from the University of North Florida.

Jessica is also an entrepreneur and philanthropist. She founded a business for marketing services and established a nonprofit for bear conservation, merging her professional skills with her passion for wildlife.

References

Niazi, P., Alimyar, O., Azizi, A., Monib, A. W., & Ozturk, H. (2023). People-plant Interaction: Plant Impact on Humans and Environment. *Journal of Environmental and Agricultural Studies*, 492), 01-07. https://doi.org/10.32996/jeas.2023.4.2.1

Howell, A. H., Völkner, C., McGreevy, P. *et al.* Pavement cells distinguish touch from letting go. *Nat. Plants* 9, 877-882 (2023).